# PRAYER FOR THE SOULS OF UNBORN BABIES

Compiled by Thich Nu Gioi Huong

# PRAYER FOR THE SOULS OF UNBORN BABIES
## (Miscarriage, Abortion, Termination, Stillbirth)

Compiled by
**Thich Nu Gioi Huong**

HƯƠNG SEN
Publishing

Contact:

**HƯƠNG SEN BUDDHIST TEMPLE**

19865 Seaton Avenue, Perris, CA 92570, USA

Tel: 951-657-7272, Cell: 951-616-8620

Email: huongsentemple@gmail.com,

thichnugioihuong@yahoo.com

Facebook:https://www.facebook.com/huongsentemple

Web: www.huongsentemple.com

Second edition 2024 Huong Sen Buddhist Temple

# CONTENTS

# Namo Kṣitigarbha Bodhisattva Mahasattva

# 1. MEANING OF PRAYER FOR THE SOULS OF UNBORN BABIES
## (Leader's Remarks)

*Prayer for the Souls of Unborn Babies* is a ritual held to pray for the souls of those little ones who did not have the chance to be born or died shortly after birth. Those souls are pure, having not yet experienced life's troubles and attachments. The temple or the family should prepare an altar with flowers, fruits, milk, and water. On the altar for the souls, there should be a memorial tablet (*with the name, Dharma name, birth date, death date and death place of the unborn babies*), three bowls of porridge, three glasses of milk, flowers, and fruits...

Offerings should be made continuously for 21 days after the passing away of the unborn child, or on the 1st and 15th day of the lunar month, or the Vu Lan Festival, Lunar New Year, death anniversaries, etc. When visiting the temple, incense should be lit, sutras recited, and prayers offered to the little ones.

When an abortion or termination is intentional, the unborn child often experiences pain and may develop feelings of resentment and sadness towards their parents.

In cases of unintentional incidents, such as

carelessness leading to complications during childbirth, miscarriage, stillbirth, or the death of a newborn at 1, 2, or 3 weeks/months, the unborn child experiences pain and anger. They may also develop attachment to their parents and family, not wanting to be separated.

Due to the livelihood needs, some people engage in professions such as performing abortions, selling abortion tools and medications, thereby creating conditions for the karmic killing, causing numerous innocent unborn children to be unjustly killed.

Today, we sincerely repent, recite sutras, resolve resentments, chant the Buddha's name and pray for the divine power of the Buddhas, Bodhisattvas, saints, Dharma protectors, and heavenly beings to bless the souls.

We pray that the unborn children release their feelings of resentment and attachment, awaken to their current circumstances, understand the impermanent nature of existence, accept reality, and soon be reborn into a peaceful realm.

# 2. INCENSE OFFERING

*(Kneel straight, hold 3 incense sticks
at forehead level; only the leader recites)*

We sincerely offer this precious incense
To all the Buddhas
To the revered Dharma, the Bodhisattvas,
the Sravakas and the Pratyekabuddhas,
and all the saints and sages.

The cause arises, the bright platform shines
Fragrance spreads across the ten directions
Permeating all sentient beings
Inspiring them to awaken the Bodhi mind
To abandon all false karma
And to fully attain the Supreme Path
Namo the Incense Offering Bodhisattva Mahasattva

(o) (1 bow down)

# 3. INTRODUCTION

### *(Explanation of the ritual)*
### *(The leader kneels before the Buddha, holds incense, and reads aloud)*

Today, on the date of .............., the grieving family, including both sides of the extended family, represented by ........... at the address ............, earnestly requests the sangha of Huong Sen Temple in Perris, California, to perform a ritual to pray for the soul of the unborn child, a girl/boy named ............................... with the Dharma name .........................., who died in the womb/shortly after birth/at ....... weeks/months of age.

The soul of the unborn child, due to karmic conditions, has (*been aborted, terminated, miscarried, resulted in stillbirth, died in the womb, or died shortly after birth, or at 1, 2, 3 weeks/ months of age*) ....... The unborn child may have experienced pain, sorrow, anger, and attachment to their parents and family lineage, without wanting to be separated.

We respectfully invite the soul of the unborn child named ..................., with the Dharma name ........................, along with all the souls in the spiritual realm, to descend and participate in the memorial service at Huong Sen Temple today.

The family of the unborn child has made offerings of flowers and fruits to the Ten Directions' Three Jewels and sincerely recites sutras, chants the Buddha's name, offers milk, cakes and porridge to the unborn children, and dedicates the merits to them.

We pray for the spirits of the unborn child, as well as all beings born from wombs, eggs, transformation or moisture, and all those in the spiritual realm to quickly find the path to liberation, escape from delusion, emerge from darkness, and be reborn in the Pure Land.

We respectfully invite the Buddhas, Bodhisattvas, Dharma protectors, heavenly beings, and deities to support this memorial service.

At this time, we invite all beings in the spiritual realm to join us in bowing to the Buddha, reciting sutras, and listening to the Dharma to awaken to the impermanence, suffering, emptiness and nonself of this world.

May we all release our attachments and aspire towards rebirth in the Pure and Peaceful Realm.

**Namo the Great Compassionate and Great Mercy, Amitabha Buddha, Teacher of the Western Pure Land, for witnessing this event.**

(o) (1 bow down)

# 4. PARENTS' REPENTANCE TO THE SOULS OF UNBORN BABIES

Today, at Huong Sen Temple, Perris, California, on the date of ................., I, named ................., am the father/mother/grandmother/grandfather/ representative of the unborn child named ..............., with the Dharma name .................... .

We have prepared a modest offering of incense, flowers, and other offerings with sincere hearts to perform a memorial service for the soul of the unborn child and to make a repentance ceremony before the Buddhas and the unborn child.

Dear Soul of the Unborn Child,

We, the parents, are deeply sorry for our actions:

Due to negligence and lack of care during pregnancy, we faced complications, miscarriages, stillbirths or other issues, leading to your departure before birth. (*Or, due to impulsiveness, ignorance, cruelty, or shallow understanding, we performed an abortion or termination, preventing you from being born...*). The parents and family are very sorrowful, regretful, and troubled for not fulfilling our duty to give you the opportunity to live as a human being. We acknowledge the pain, suffering, hunger, torment, loneliness and helplessness you endured.

Now that you have departed, it is a harsh reality that we, as your parents, must accept. The separation from you is due to the insufficient karmic conditions between us in this life.

We hope you understand the heartfelt sorrow of your parents and do not harbor resentment, create karmic bonds, or cling to us. Please accept your current karma and release any worldly attachments. If this lifetime has not provided sufficient conditions, we hope to have the opportunity in future lives when our karmic connections are complete. We sincerely repent to the Buddhas and you.

May you rely on the divine power of the Buddhas, take refuge in the Three Jewels, and follow the path of love and understanding, avoiding the dark realms of hell, hungry ghosts, and animals.

Together with the esteemed nuns of Huong Sen Temple, and with your parents and family, we focus our minds on reciting the Buddha's name, listening to the sutras, and praying for you to be reborn in the Pure Land or in a truly peaceful and happy realm.

**Namo the Repentance Bodhisattva Mahasatva (o)**

**Namo the Witnessing Bodhisattvas (ooo)**

# 5. PRAISING THE BUDDHAS

The Supreme Dharma King in the three realms
Teaches throughout heaven and earth
A benevolent Father to all beings
Refuge is completed with a single mind.


Eradicating all karma from the three periods
We extol and praise
Admiration in boundless eons. (o) (1 bow down)


The Buddha and beings have the same eternal
stillness nature
The Way is profound and beyond
conceptualization.
The jewel net represents the Dharma realm
The Buddhas in ten directions shine with the
radiant light.
Before the sacred seat, our form appears
We bow our head and vow to take refuge.
(o) (1 bow down)

# 6. PROSTRATING TO BUDDHAS AND BODHISATTVAS

*(Everyone recites together)*

With utmost sincerity, we pay homage:

**Namo all Buddhas in the past, present, future of the ten directions**

**Permeating the Dharma realm from the end of the cosmos**

**The perpetual Three Jewels of the Noble Dharma, the Noble Sangha.** (o) (1 prostrate)

With utmost sincerity, we pay homage:

**Namo Shakyamuni Buddha, the Founder of the Dharma in the Saha world**

**To Maitreya Buddha, the Buddha-to-be**

**To Manjushri Bodhisattva, the Great Wisdom**

**To Samantabhadra Bodhisattva, the Great Practice**

**To the Dharma-protecting Bodhisattvas**

**And to the Bodhisattvas and Buddhas of the Lingshan Assembly.**

(o) (1 prostrate)

With utmost sincerity, we pay homage:

**Namo Amitabha Buddha of the Western Pure Land, the Great Compassionate and Merciful One,**

**To Avalokiteshvara Bodhisattva, the Great Compassion,**

**To Mahasthamaprapta Bodhisattva, the Great Power of Aspiration,**

**To Ksitigarbha Bodhisattva, the Great Vow,**

**And to the Bodhisattvas of the Great Ocean of Purity.** (o) (1 prostrate)

# 7. BEGINNING RITUAL VERSE
*(Please sit down and strike the bell with gong)*

**The magical pure water of poplar branches**

**sprinkles away countless sufferings**

**The heavenly beings are cool, their minds are pure**

**The human world is happy, the scene is peaceful**

**Nectar sprinkled all over the world**

**The anger fire is completely extinguished, the golden lotus blooms.**

**Namo Pure Water Bodhisattva Mahasattva**

(3 times) (o)

# 8. UNBORN BABIES TAKE REFUGE IN THE THREE JEWELS

We perform the ceremony of Refuge for the souls of the unborn children, guiding them to rely on the Buddha (*the one who shows the way*), the Dharma (*the path of love and understanding*), and the Sangha (*the pure community that guides and supports on the path of practice*) so that the unborn child and the deceased in all realms may receive blessings and be reborn in a better realm.

The family, in place of the unborn child, will carry out the ceremony of taking refuge. Please join us in reciting the following three vows with reverence:

**The unborn child named .... takes refuge in the Buddha, who guides them on their path in life.** (o)

**The unborn child named .... takes refuge in the Dharma, the path of love and understanding.** (o)

**The unborn child named .... takes refuge in the Sangha, the community of those who aspire to live a mindful life.** (ooo)

**The unborn child takes refuge in the Buddha.** (o)

The unborn child takes refuge in the Dharma. (o)

The unborn child takes refuge in the Sangha. (ooo)

The unborn child takes refuge in the Buddha, the one of perfect blessing and wisdom. (o)

The unborn child takes refuge in the Dharma, the path that transcends desire and attachment. (o)

The unborn child takes refuge in the Sangha, the highest practitioners. (ooo)

The unborn child takes refuge in the Buddha, with the vow to never take refuge in deities, spirits, or demonic beings. (o)

The unborn child takes refuge in the Dharma, with the vow to never follow heretical or false teachings. (o)

The unborn child takes refuge in the Sangha, with the vow to never follow harmful or wicked sects. (ooo)

Leader:

Good fortune! From now on, these unborn children have officially taken refuge in the Three Jewels, accepting the Three Precious Jewels into their consciousness with the Dharma name of ........... The unborn children have become disciples of the Enlightened One and have vowed to live according to the path of mindfulness and liberation taught by the Buddha. (o)

Starting today, the consciousness of these unborn children will rely on the temple for practice, listening to teachings, and reciting sutras to transform anger, attachment and ignorance into love, forgiveness, compassion and wisdom in this life and many future lives. (ooo)

# 9. UNBORN BABIES DEVELOP THE BODHI MIND

Sentient beings are countless;
we vow to save them.

Afflictions are endless;
we vow to eradicate them.

The Dharma doors are immeasurable;
we vow to learn them.

The Buddha Way is supreme;
we vow to attain it. (3 times) (o)

The nature of sentient beings;
we vow to realize it.

**The nature of afflictions;
we vow to eradicate them.**

**The nature of the Dharma doors;
we vow to learn them.**

**The nature of the Buddha Way;
we vow to attain it**. (3 times) (o)

The leader reads:

**May the Buddhas in the past, present, and future of the ten directions who pervade the infinite Dharma realm, the Noble Dharma and the Noble Sangha who are eternally abiding in the Three Jewels, guide the unborn child named .........., with the Dharma name .......... All together: May they be reborn in the Pure Land of Ultimate Bliss.** (Family members bow down) (o)

**May the Tathagata Shakyamuni Buddha, the Compassionate and Merciful Teacher of the Saha world, the Maitreya Buddha, Manjushri Bodhisattva, the embodiment of Great Wisdom, Samantabhadra Bodhisattva, the embodiment of Great Practice, the Buddhas and Bodhisattvas of the Lingshan Assembly, guide the unborn child named .........., with the Dharma name .......... All together read: May they be reborn in the Pure Land of Ultimate Bliss.** (Family members bow down) (o)

May Amitabha Buddha, the Great Compassionate and Merciful Teacher of the Western Pure Land; Avalokiteshvara Bodhisattva, the embodiment of Great Compassion, Mahasthamaprapta Bodhisattva, the embodiment of Great Aspiration, and Ksitigarbha Bodhisattva, the embodiment of Great Vows, guide the unborn child named .......... with the Dharma name .......... All together read: **May they be reborn in the Pure Land of Ultimate Bliss.** (Family members bow down) (o)

# 10. OPENING SUTRA VERSE

**Dharma is so wondrous, profound and lofty**

**In countless eons, it is hard to seek.**

**Now we hear and recite it with utmost sincerity,**

**We vow to understand the profound meaning of the Tathagata.**

**Namo the Original Teacher Shakyamuni Buddha.** (3 times) (o)

# 11. CHANTING

*(Next, strike the bell and gong.*

*Recite one, two, or all five sutras,*
*depending on the time available)*


Sutra 1: Loving-Kindness Sutra (Metta Sutra)

Sutra 2: Sutra on Consequences of Good and Evil Deeds

Sutra 3: Sutra on Karmic Retribution of Hungry Ghosts

Sutra 4: Sutra on Longevity and Shortened Life


## 11.1. LOVING-KINDNESS SUTRA (METTA SUTRA)

Someone who wants to attain peace should practice being upright, humble, and capable of using loving speech. They will know how to live simply and happily, with senses calmed, without being covetous and carried away by the emotions of the majority. Let them not do anything that will be disapproved of by the wise ones. (o)

And this is what they contemplate:

May everyone be happy and safe, and may all hearts be filled with joy.

May all beings live in security and in peace –

beings who are frail or strong, tall or short, big or small, invisible or visible, near or faraway, already born, or yet to be born. May all of them dwell in perfect tranquility.

Let no one do harm to anyone. Let no one put the life of anyone in danger. Let no one, out of anger or ill will, wish anyone any harm.

Just as a mother loves and protects her only child at the risk of her own life, cultivate boundless love to offer to all living beings in the entire cosmos. (o)

Let our boundless love pervade the whole universe, above, below, and across. Our love will know no obstacles. Our heart will be absolutely free from hatred and enmity. Whether standing or walking, sitting or lying, as long as we are awake, we should maintain this mindfulness of love in our own heart. This is the noblest way of living.

Free from wrong views, greed, and sensual desires, living in beauty and realizing Perfect Understanding, those who practice boundless love will certainly transcend birth and death."[1] (ooo)

---

1. Translated by Thich Nhat Hanh from the Mettā Sutta, Sutta Nipāta 1.8.
For commentary, see Thich Nhat Hanh, *Teachings on Love* (Berkeley, CA: Parallax Press, 1998).

## 11.2. SUTRA ON CONSEQUENCES OF GOOD AND EVIL DEEDS

I heard that at one time the Buddha was in the city of Shravasti, in the garden of Anathapindika, within the grove of Prince Jeta. (o)

At that time, as the World-Honored One was teaching the Dharma, there were countless Bodhisattvas, gods, and beings from the human realm surrounding Him, all attentively and silently listening. At that moment, I, Ananda, asked the Buddha on behalf of sentient beings, saying: "Revered World-Honored One! In this world, among those born into human existence, there are those who are beautiful and those who are unattractive, the strong and the weak, the poor and the rich, the suffering and the joyful, the noble and the humble. The sounds and languages differ; some people live a long life of a hundred years, while others die at thirty, some at fifteen, and even infants who fall into misfortune while still in the womb. There are those who are dignified, and those who are humble, some who are unattractive yet wealthy, and others who are very healthy yet of low status. Some are weak yet rise to high positions, some suffer but live long, some are joyful yet die early. There are those who do good but encounter many misfortunes, while those who commit evil receive benefits. Some who are fat and pale have crossed eyes, while those who are dark-skinned are beautiful. Some, despite being short, possess great ambition, while others, though tall, end up as servants in lowly positions. Some have many sons and daughters, while others are solitary. There are those who leave their homes and wander in poverty, while some live in palaces and enjoy luxurious clothing. Some are poor in youth but become wealthy in old age, while others who are truly innocent are imprisoned. There are families with filial children and harmonious relationships, studying scriptures and explaining meanings, while others face discord and strife. Some have well-established homes and abundant wealth, while others have no house and wander from place to place, living a precarious and miserable life. Some live like scavengers or wild animals, while others consume raw meat and drink blood, wearing animal skins and knowing nothing of letters. Some live comfortably enjoying their blessings, while others seek work but cannot find employment. Some are intelligent and enlightened, while others are ignorant and foolish. Some succeed in business, while others find wealth coming to them without effort. Some are wealthy but greedy, while others are poor yet generous. (o)

Some speak sweetly, while others speak with sharpness; some are loved by many, while others are shunned by everyone. Some are compassionate and care for all living beings, while others kill without mercy. Some are tolerant and gain the favor of others, while others are neglected by the people.

In some households, the daughter-in-law and mother-in-law despise each other, while in others, the sisters-in-law live harmoniously together. Some eagerly listen to teachings, while others fall asleep during the recitation. Some are rude and unrefined, while others are diligent in studying literature. Some mimic the mannerisms of animals. I ask the World-Honored One to elaborate on the laws of cause and effect for us, so that we may sincerely practice virtue.

Then the World-Honored One said to Ananda: "As you have inquired, the different conditions of sentient beings arise from their actions in past lives, which is why there are so many variations. Those who are now blessed with good appearance and disposition have practiced patience and virtue in past lives. (o)

Those who are now ugly were previously characterized by anger and irritation. Those who are now poor had a tendency towards greed and miserliness in past lives. Those who are now noble and esteemed practiced reverence for the Buddhas in their past lives.

Those who are now lowly had a nature of arrogance in their past lives. Those who are tall and dignified were respectful in past lives, while those who are short and unremarkable exhibited arrogance towards the Dharma in their previous lives." (o)

Those who are arrogant and unruly are the result of having been goats in past lives.

Those who are are dismal and unattractive had obscured the light of the Buddha in their previous lives.

Those who have a stiff tongue had tasted forbidden offerings in past lives.

Those with red eyes were miserly and begrudging with light in their previous lives.

Those who are blind today had previously been involved in harming birds and their eyes.

Those who are mute or have speech difficulties in this life had slandered the Dharma in their previous lives.

Those who are deaf and hard of hearing now did not enjoy hearing the Dharma in their past lives.

Those who have missing teeth in this life had

previously consumed bones and meat.

Those who have blocked noses in this life had offered bad incense to the Buddha in their previous lives. (o)

Those who have cleft lips in this life had previously pierced or cut the lips or gills of fish.

Those with yellowish skin had shaved the hair of pigs in their past lives.

Those with elongated ears had previously pierced the ears of living beings.

Those with disfigured bodies had worn thin clothes and stood before statues of the Buddha and Bodhisattvas in their past lives.

Those who are lame today had seen their teachers and elders without standing up in their past lives.

Those with hunched backs today had previously worn thin clothing and turned their backs on the Buddha.

Those with low or protruding foreheads today had previously failed to bow respectfully before the Buddha and had knocked their foreheads with their hands. (o)

Those with retracted necks today had previously seen their elders or teachers retreating and fleeing.

Those with heart conditions today had previously inflicted harm on the bodies of living beings.

Those with leprosy today had previously deceived and stolen from others.

Those with coughs and respiratory problems today had given people cold food in the harsh winter.

Those without children today had previously raised and cared for animals. (o)

Those who live long today had shown compassion in their previous lives.

Those who die young today had previously been involved in killing living beings.

Those who are wealthy today had practiced generosity and charity in their past lives.

Those who have carriages or horses today had previously made offerings to the Three Jewels with carriages or horses. (o)

Those who are intelligent today had previously been eager to learn and recite scriptures.

Those who are dull-witted today had previously been reborn as animals.

Those who are in servitude today had previously been poor but sought after official positions.

Those who dance or move about erratically today had previously been reborn as monkeys.

Those who suffer from leprosy today had previously harmed the Three Jewels.

Those with twisted limbs today had previously bound the limbs of living beings.

Those with a malicious nature today had previously been reborn as snakes, scorpions, or centipedes. (o)

Those with all six senses fully developed today had previously diligently observed precepts.

Those with impaired senses today-ears, eyes, nose, tongue, body and mind-had previously broken precepts.

Those who live in filth today had previously been reborn as pigs.

Those who are fond of singing and dancing today had previously been entertainers or performers in their past lives.

Those who are excessively greedy today were previously reborn as dogs.

Those who have a fleshy protrusion hanging from their necks (like a double chin) today had previously been greedy and ate alone.

Those who have foul breath today had previously been harsh or abusive in their speech …

Those with short, speech-impaired tongues today had previously sat in secluded places, mocking or insulting elders.

Those who are lustful towards others' wives today may be reborn as ducks or geese in their next life.

Those who engage in self-indulgence or self-abuse today may be reborn as peacocks or sparrows.

Those who hoard or conceal wisdom and refuse to share it with others may be reborn as wood-boring insects (like termites).

Those who are fond of using weapons and hunting may be reborn among primitive or savage tribes.

Those who are violent and kill animals may be reborn as fierce predators (like tigers, leopards, or wolves). (o)

Those who wear garlands or adornments inappropriately may be reborn as insects with floral patterns.

Those who habitually wear long, flowing robes may be reborn as insects with long tails.

Those who lie down while eating may be reborn as pigs.

Those who enjoy wearing brightly colored,

flashy clothes may be reborn as birds with bright, patterned feathers. (o)

Those who imitate or mock people's speech or mannerisms may be reborn as parrots.

Those who mock or ridicule others may be reborn as venomous snakes.

Those who cause others to feel sorrow or distress may be reborn as painful, distressing insects.

Those who spread harmful rumors or deceit may be reborn as owls or hawks.

Those who cause others to be falsely accused or imprisoned may be reborn as wild beasts.

Those who induce great fear or terror in others may be reborn as deer or elk.

Those who previously wore wooden sandals or shoes in temples may now be reborn as creatures with hooves like horses. (o)

Those who previously emitted foul odors may now be reborn as insects that produce unpleasant smells.

Those who previously forced others to eat less may now be reborn as wood-boring insects.

Those who used pestles to grind food for the monastics may now be reborn as head-down insects.

Those who live as fish in this life, have done so because they misused the water of the monastics in a previous life.

Those who pollute the land where the monastics live, will be reborn as insects in filthy places.

Those who steal fruits or vegetables belonging to the monastics, will be reborn as insects that feed on mud or dirt.

Those who in a previous life stole from the monastics, will be reborn as oxen or donkeys used for grinding. (o)

Those who previously extorted from the monastics will be reborn as white doves.

Those who previously insulted the monastics will be reborn as insects that infest the necks of oxen.

Those who abused the vegetables of the monastics will be reborn as worms in bitter vegetables.

Those who showed disrespect by sitting on the monastic's bed will be reborn as eels or leeches.

Those who misused the monastic's possessions will be reborn as fireflies.

Those who spit or expectorate in the temple grounds will be reborn as long-beaked birds.

Those who wear striped or flashy makeup and adornments in the temple will be reborn as red-beaked birds. (o)

Those who wear brightly colored clothing in the temple will be reborn as colorful birds.

In a previous life, those who slept together in the temple will be reborn as insect pests.

Those who sat on or trampled upon stupas in a previous life will be reborn as camels.

Those who entered temples or monasteries wearing shoes or sandals will be reborn as frogs, toads, mice, or insects.

Those who talked loudly during Dharma teachings will be reborn as long-beaked birds.

Those who defiled the purity of the monastic's practice will be reborn in the Iron Hell, where countless swords will cut their bodies in one instant. (o)

At that time, A-Nan asked the Buddha, "Revered Buddha, according to your teachings, offending the monastics is indeed a grave sin. If so, how can laypeople approach the temple with reverence and offer their respects?"

The Buddha replied, "There are two kinds of minds when people come to the temple: a benevolent mind and a malevolent mind.

What is a benevolent mind? It is when a person visits the temple, bows before the Buddha, shows respect to the monastics, inquires about the teachings, and receives precepts and engages in repentance. They contribute their wealth to build and maintain temples and support the Dharma, without sparing their lives to protect the True Teaching. Such individuals, with each step they take, ascend to heavenly realms, and in future lives, they will enjoy blessings like the tree of Bodhi. Such people are considered the most virtuous.

What is a malevolent mind? Some beings, when they go to the temple, only watch and seek to borrow money or possessions from the monastics, criticize them, point out their faults, or seek to disrupt their practices. They may consume offerings without shame-such as cakes, fruits, or vegetables-and even take them home. Such individuals will fall into the Iron Hell, where they will be punished in boiling cauldrons, fiery furnaces, or by sharp blades and swords. These are considered the most wretched of evil beings!" (o)

The Buddha also advised A-Nan: "You must admonish my future disciples that when they go to the temple, they should be very careful not to offend the possessions of the Three Jewels.

They should make every effort to show sincere respect, not falter in their devotion, and listen to the Buddha's teachings. When Maitreya Buddha appears in the future, they will undoubtedly be saved and freed."

The Buddha said: "In this life, those who steal or rob others' clothes will fall into the Ice Hell, and later be reborn as silkworms, subjected to being boiled and spun for silk.

Those who refuse to light lamps for reading the sutras or making offerings to the images will fall into the Dark Hell in the Iron Mountain.

Those who are butchers, killing living beings, will fall into the Hell of Sword Mountain and Knife Tree.

Those who are addicted to hunting, using dogs or falcons as prey, will fall into the Hell of Iron Cages.

Those who engage in immoral sexual conduct will fall into the Hell of Copper Pillars and Iron Bed after death."

In this life, those who keep many wives will fall into the Iron Gate Hell after death.

Those who keep many husbands will fall into the Poisonous Snake Hell after death.

Those who roast chickens will fall into the Smelly River Hell after death. (o)

Those who pluck feathers from chickens or shave pigs will fall into the Hell of Foul Water after death.

Those who castrate dogs or pigs will fall into the Stone Needle Hell after death.

Those who drink alcohol and get drunk will fall into the Hell of Drinking Copper Water after death.

Those who cut and injure living beings will fall into the Hell of Iron Wheels after death.

Those who steal fruits from the monastics will fall into the Iron Ring Hell after death.

Those who consume the entrails of dogs or pigs will fall into the Hell of Excrement and Urine after death.

Those who eat raw fish will fall into the Hell of Sword Mountains and Tree Blades after death.

Those who are cruel stepmothers to their stepchildren will fall into the Hell of Fire Wheels after death.

Those who speak deceitfully to incite conflicts among people will fall into the Hell of Iron Cranes after death.

Those who speak maliciously and insult others will fall into the Hell of Flayed Tongues after death.

Those who frequently lie will fall into the Hell of Crushed Tongues after death. (o)

Those who kill living beings to offer to false gods will fall into the Hell of Iron Moats after death.

Those who pretend to be mediums or shamans, deceiving people with fake messages from spirits to take their money, will fall into the Hell of Flesh Mountains after death.

Those who pretend to be mediums, closing their eyes and looking down while pretending to communicate with spirits to deceive people, will fall into the Hell of Cross-cutting (where bodies are cut in half) after death.

Those who act as mediums, instructing people to kill beings for offerings to great gods or to avert disasters, including gods of earth, deities, or local spirits, will fall into the Hell of Deception after death. There, they will be subjected to being sliced, chopped, and dissected by demons, and pecked by iron-beaked birds who will gouge out their eyes. (o)

Those who practice divination, astrology, or fortune-telling, or who engage in false predictions about tomb placement, family affairs, and fortunes to deceive people and take their money, will fall into the Hell of Iron Beaks after death.

In this hell, numerous birds will perch on them, pecking at their flesh and gnawing at their bones, enduring immense suffering. (o)

Those who destroy temples and pagodas, deceive monks, or are unfilial to their parents will fall into the Great Hell of Avici, passing through eight major hells and many minor ones, suffering for one hundred thirty-six eons, from one eon to five eons. Only after that can they be released, provided they encounter virtuous teachers and cultivate the Bodhi mind; otherwise, they will fall back into hell."

The Buddha said: "Those who are born with a very foul and dirty body and a heart full of anger and resentment are those who, in their previous lives, were reborn as camels.

Those who travel frequently, eat heartily, and do not avoid dangers and difficulties were previously reborn as horses. (o)

Those who endure harsh weather and are forgetful were previously reborn as oxen.

Those who speak loudly, are shameless, and are driven by desires without discerning right from wrong were previously reborn as donkeys.

Those who are greedy for meat, do not fear any challenges, were previously reborn as lions.

Those with long hair, small eyes, and a

tendency to avoid staying in one place were previously reborn as birds.

Those who are strong and robust, who are not overly interested in sexual matters, and who do not love their family, were previously reborn as wolves.

Those who do not care for beautiful clothing, are prone to catching thieves, have little sleep, and are often angry, were previously reborn as dogs.

Those who are passionate about sexual matters, talk a lot, and are loved by many, were previously reborn as parrots.

Those who find joy in crowds and speak in a troublesome manner were previously reborn as mynah birds.

Those who are small in stature, have a strong sexual appetite, lack focus, and are captivated by physical beauty, were previously reborn as sparrows.

Those who have red eyes, short teeth, froth at the mouth while speaking, and curl up when lying down, were previously reborn as snakes or pythons.

Those who speak with a temper, do not consider the meaning or reason, and breathe out poisonous fire, were previously reborn as scorpions, centipedes, or wood-boring insects. (o)

Those who eat alone and sleep little at night were previously reborn as frogs.

Those who dig into walls and theft, are greedy and full of resentment, with no concern for family or friends, were previously reborn as rats."

The Buddha said: "Those who destroy temples and stupas or hide the offerings of the Triple Gem for their own use, will be condemned to the great hell of Avici. After being released from hell, they will be reborn as animals such as pigeons, sparrows, mandarin ducks, nightingales, peacocks, fish, monkeys, gibbons, deer, or if they are reborn as humans, they will face the plight of being an outcast or a person with physical defects such as eunuchs or those lacking proper organs. (o)

Those who are prone to anger will be reborn as poisonous snakes, lions, tigers, leopards, bears, cats, wolves, or eagles. If they are reborn as humans, they may be involved in activities such as raising chickens and pigs, slaughtering animals, hunting, fishing, or serving as jailers.

Those who encounter the Buddha's teachings but remain ignorant of the Dharma will be reborn as elephants, pigs, cattle, goats, water buffaloes, lice, fleas, flies, mosquitoes, ants, or in other lowly forms. If they are reborn as humans, they may be blind, deaf, mute, have speech impediments, or be physically deformed, lacking the ability to receive teachings.

Those who are arrogant will be reborn as insects in dung heaps, or as burden-carrying mules, dogs, or horses. If they are reborn as humans, they may become impoverished servants or beggars, and be despised by others. (o)

Those who, in their lifetime, hold positions of power and are greedy for the people's wealth will be condemned to the hell of Flesh Mountain after death, where countless demons will cut and eat their flesh.

Those who break the precepts by eating at night will, after death, be reborn as hungry ghosts, suffering from extreme hunger and thirst for countless years, with flames spewing from their mouths as they walk.

Those who indulge in sitting shirtless will, after death, be reborn as cold-dwelling insects.

Those who take leftover offerings from monks for their own consumption will be condemned to the hell of Flesh Iron, and when reborn as humans, they will suffer from diseases like diphtheria and die young.

Those who do not place their head on the

ground while bowing to the Buddha will be condemned to the hell of Reversal of Destiny, and when reborn as humans, they will often be deceived.

Those who do not clasp their hands together while bowing to the Buddha will be reborn in border regions, where they will experience many hardships and few gains. (o)

Those who fail to rise when they hear the sound of the temple bell will be reborn as large snakes, their bodies infested with worms.

Those who clasp their hands together but do so in a non-reverent manner while bowing to the Buddha, will be condemned to the hell of Reversal of Fate, and when reborn as humans, they will encounter many evils.

Those who bow to the Buddha with both hands clasped and their whole body prostrated to the ground with utmost sincerity will be reborn in noble families, enjoying happiness and comfort in the future.

Those who are prone to anger and sorrow are said to be experiencing the result of having been mentally disturbed in their previous lives.

Those whose pupils are misaligned (strabismus) are experiencing the result of having spied on women in their previous lives. (o)

Those who favor their wives and scold their parents will, after death, be condemned to the hell of Tongue-Slicing.

Those who dilute wine with water and sell it to others will be reborn as water-dwelling insects, and when reborn as humans, will suffer from diseases like ulcers and shortness of breath."

The Buddha then taught A-Nan: "The suffering I have described arises from the ten evil actions. High suffering is the result of actions leading to hell; medium suffering comes from actions leading to rebirth as animals; and low suffering results from actions leading to rebirth as hungry ghosts. (o)

The sin of killing causes beings to be reborn in hell as hungry ghosts, or as animals, and if reborn as humans, they will face two types of consequences: early death and numerous illnesses.

The sin of theft also results in rebirth in hell, as hungry ghosts, or as animals, and if reborn as humans, they will face two types of consequences: poverty and restrictions on their possessions.

The sin of sexual misconduct leads to rebirth in hell, as hungry ghosts, or as animals, and if reborn as humans, they will face two types of consequences: unfaithful wives and disputes among wives.

The sin of lying causes beings to be reborn in hell as hungry ghosts, or as animals. If reborn as humans, they will face two types of consequences: one is frequent slander by others, and the other is being often deceived by others. (o)

The sin of causing discord (sowing division) leads beings to rebirth in hell, as hungry ghosts, or as animals. If reborn as humans, they will face two types of consequences: one is having their family disrupted, and the other is having malevolent relatives.

The sin of harsh speech causes beings to be reborn in hell, as hungry ghosts, or as animals. If reborn as humans, they will face two types of consequences: one is constantly hearing harsh words, and the other is being involved in disputes and legal conflicts.

The sin of flattery or deceitful speech causes beings to be reborn in hell, as hungry ghosts, or as animals. If reborn as humans, they will face two types of consequences: one is having their words not believed, and the other is their speech being unclear or ambiguous.

The sin of greed and lust causes beings to be reborn in hell as hungry ghosts, or as animals. If reborn as humans, they will face two types of consequences: one is insatiable greed for wealth, and the other is unfulfilled desires and numerous disappointments. (o)

The sin of anger causes beings to be reborn in hell as hungry ghosts, or as animals. If reborn as humans, they will face two types of consequences: one is frequent criticism and blame from others, and the other is suffering from harmful actions inflicted by others.

The sin of wrong views causes beings to be reborn in hell as hungry ghosts, or as animals. If reborn as humans, they will face two types of consequences: one is often being born into families with wrong views, and the other is having a deceitful and insincere nature. The followers of the Buddha should understand that such evil karma brings immense suffering and constitutes a major cause of suffering."

At that time, in the assembly, someone who had committed the ten evil deeds, upon hearing the Buddha describe the sufferings of hell, cried out in fear and asked the Buddha, saying:

"Venerable Master, what practices should we undertake to escape from such suffering? We humbly request your guidance."

The Buddha replied: "You should teach all beings to cultivate virtuous deeds. What are virtuous deeds? If any beings today serve as major benefactors by constructing temples, stupas, or monastic residences, they will receive the merit of becoming kings in future lives, ruling over many lands and having people submit to them.

Those who serve as regional leaders or officials today will be reborn as ministers or high-ranking officials in their next lives, enjoying great honor and prestige. Those who encourage many people to perform acts of merit will be reborn as wealthy and respected elders in the future, with their paths always open and prosperous.

Those who light lamps and keep the light burning today will be reborn in the celestial realm of Sun and Moonlight, where they will shine brightly.

Those who practice generosity and compassion, nurturing life, will be reborn in wealthy and prosperous places, where they will naturally have fine clothing and comfort.

Those who provide food and drink to others will enjoy the following benefits: providing food to animals will result in a hundredfold reward, while providing food to monks will yield a thousandfold reward.

Offering to monks who uphold precepts will bring a myriad of benefits. Offering to Dharma teachers who propagate the Great Vehicle and reveal the profound teachings of the Tathagata will bring boundless rewards, opening the eyes and hearts of many. Offering to Bodhisattvas and Buddhas will result in immense merit. Offering to three groups of people brings inexhaustible blessings: one is the Buddhas, two is parents, and three is those who are ill.

A single offering of food can bring limitless merit. If such offerings are made regularly, the blessings will never be exhausted.

Those who wash and bathe the monks today will be reborn in places where clothing and adornments come naturally, with respect from others, and with a dignified appearance and radiant face.

Those who praise the Buddha and are fond of reciting the Dharma will have harmonious and pleasing voices in their future lives, bringing joy to all who hear them.

Those who keep precepts today will be reborn with a dignified and noble demeanor, standing out as the finest among humans.

Those who dig wells, provide jars or water containers for others, or plant trees along the road for people to rest under will be reborn as kings in any place they are born, with all kinds of food and drink readily available.

Those who write and copy the Dharma texts for others to read will have eloquent and versatile speech in their future lives, mastering any subject they hear just once. They will receive the constant blessings of Buddhas and Bodhisattvas, standing out as the finest among humans and often becoming leaders.

Those who build bridges or ferry people across rivers will be reborn with all seven treasures in any place they are born, receiving admiration and respect from others, and will be supported and honored wherever they go." (o)

At this point, Ananda asked the Buddha: "O World-Honored One, what is the name of this sutra and how should it be practiced? Please kindly instruct us."

The Buddha replied to Ananda: "This sutra is called the 'Karma of Good and Evil' or the 'Bodhisattva's Vows and Practices.' One should accept and uphold it in this manner."

When the Buddha finished speaking the sutra, among the assembly of eighty thousand people, there were many who aspired to the Anuttara Samyak Sambodhi (Supreme Perfect Enlightenment) . . . . One thousand two hundred evildoers abandoned their malicious intentions and realized their previous lives. Countless celestial beings and humans attained the Non-Birth Patience and enjoyed perpetual bliss. Countless listeners were reborn in the Pure Lands and became companions of Buddhas and Bodhisattvas. All the assembly returned home to practice virtue, joyfully chanting and practicing.[2] (o)

## 11.3. SUTRA ON KARMIC RETRIBUTION OF HUNGRY GHOSTS

At one time, the Venerable Maha Moggallana was residing with the Buddha at Vulture Peak Mountain and then traveled to the banks of the Ganges River. There, he observed numerous hungry ghosts suffering due to their various karmic offenses. Seeing the Venerable, they respectfully approached and inquired about the reasons for their suffering. (o)

One ghost asked:

"I have this body without arms or legs, resembling a lump of flesh, living in the wilderness and being torn apart by foxes, tigers, wolves, eagles, and vultures. The pain is unbearable. What karma caused this?"

2. The Sutra on Consequences of Good and Evil Deeds. https://phatgiao.org.vn/kinh-thien-ac-nhan-qua-tieng-vi-et-d70103. html

The Venerable Maha Moggallana replied:

"In a previous life, you committed acts of killing, robbery, and harm to many lives. Due to these evil deeds, after death, you were reborn as a hungry ghost with this form, enduring pain and being torn apart by other creatures."

Another ghost then inquired:

"Venerable, my body is continuously engulfed in flames, never extinguished. I suffer immensely. What is the cause of this?" (o)

The Venerable Maha Moggallana answered:

"You once set forests on fire, killing countless living beings. These cruel actions have resulted in your current suffering, constantly being burned and in pain."

The Buddha then addressed the monks:

"These hungry ghosts are enduring such suffering due to their evil actions in past lives. Remember that every action has corresponding consequences. Strive to practice diligently and avoid committing evil deeds to escape such suffering."

When the Buddha finished speaking, the monks rejoiced and faithfully followed his teachings.[3] (ooo)

3. Sutra on the Karmic Retribution of Hungry Ghosts. Khuddaka Nikaya Petavatthu (Verses of the Hungry Ghosts)

## 11.4. SUTRA ON LONGEVITY AND SHORTENED LIFE

So I have heard. At one time the Buddha was staying near Sāvatthī in Jeta's Grove, Anathapindika's monastery. (o)

Then the brahmin student Subha, Todeyya's son, approached the Buddha, and exchanged greetings with him. When the greetings and polite conversation were over, he sat down to one side and said to the Buddha:

"What is the cause, Mister Gotama, what is the reason why even among those who are human beings some are seen to be inferior and superior? For people are seen who are short-lived and long-lived, sickly and healthy, ugly and beautiful, insignificant and illustrious, poor and rich, from low and eminent families, witless and wise. What is the reason why even among those who are human beings some are seen to be inferior and superior?"

"Student, sentient beings are the owners of their deeds and heir to their deeds. Deeds are their womb, their relative, and their refuge. It is deeds that divide beings into inferior and superior. (o)

"I don't understand the meaning of what Mister Gotama has said in brief, without

https://www.accesstoinsight.org/tipitaka/kn/pv/index.html

54

explaining the details. Mister Gotama, please teach me this matter in detail so I can understand the meaning."

"Well then, student, listen and apply your mind well, I will speak."

"'Yes, sir,' replied Subha. The Buddha said this:

"Take some woman or man who kills living creatures. They're violent, bloody handed, a hardened killer, merciless to living beings. Because of undertaking such deeds, when their body breaks up, after death, they're reborn in a place of loss, a bad place, the underworld, hell. If they're not reborn in a place of loss, but return to the human realm, then wherever they're reborn they're short-lived. For killing living creatures is the path leading to a short lifespan.

But take some woman or man who gives up killing living creatures. They renounce the rod and the sword. They're scrupulous and kind, living full of sympathy for all living beings. Because of undertaking such deeds, when their body breaks up, after death, they're reborn in a good place, a heavenly realm. If they're not reborn in a heavenly realm, but return to the human realm, then wherever they're reborn they're long-lived. For not killing living creatures is the path leading to a long lifespan. (o)

Take some woman or man who habitually hurts living creatures with a fist, stone, rod, or sword. Because of undertaking such deeds, after death they're reborn in a place of loss... or if they return to the human realm, they're sickly...

But take some woman or man who would never hurt living creatures with a fist, stone, rod, or sword. Because of undertaking such deeds, after death they're reborn in a heavenly realm... or if they return to the human realm, they're healthy...

Take some woman or man who is irritable and bad-tempered. Even when lightly criticized they lose their temper, becoming annoyed, hostile, and hard-hearted, and displaying annoyance, hate, and bitterness. Because of undertaking such deeds, after death they're reborn in a place of loss... or if they return to the human realm, they're ugly...

But take some woman or man who isn't irritable and bad-tempered. Even when heavily criticized, they don't lose their temper, become annoyed, hostile, and hard-hearted, or display annoyance, hate, and bitterness. Because of undertaking such deeds, after death they're reborn in a heavenly realm... or if they return to the human realm, they're lovely...

Take some woman or man who is jealous. They

envy, resent, and begrudge the possessions, honor, respect, reverence, homage, and veneration given to others. Because of undertaking such deeds, after death they're reborn in a place of loss... or if they return to the human realm, they're insignificant...

But take some woman or man who is not jealous... Because of undertaking such deeds, after death they're reborn in a heavenly realm... or if they return to the human realm, they're illustrious...

Take some woman or man who doesn't give to ascetics or brahmins such things as food, drink, clothing, vehicles; garlands, perfumes, and makeup; and bed, house, and lighting. Because of undertaking such deeds, after death they're reborn in a place of loss... or if they return to the human realm, they're poor...

But take some woman or man who does give to ascetics or brahmins... Because of undertaking such deeds, after death they're reborn in a heavenly realm... or if they return to the human realm, they're rich...

Take some woman or man who is obstinate and vain. They don't bow to those they should bow to. They don't rise up for them, offer them a seat, make way for them, or honor, respect, esteem, or venerate those who are worthy of such. Because of undertaking such deeds, after death they're reborn in a place of loss... or if they return to the human realm, they're reborn in a low-class family...

But take some woman or man who is not obstinate and vain... Because of undertaking such deeds, after death they're reborn in a heavenly realm... or if they return to the human realm, they're reborn in an eminent family... (o)

Take some woman or man who doesn't approach an ascetic or brahmin to ask: 'Sir, what is skillful and what is unskillful? What is blameworthy and what is blameless? What should be cultivated and what should not be cultivated? What kind of action will lead to my lasting harm and suffering? Or what kind of action will lead to my lasting welfare and happiness?' Because of undertaking such deeds, after death they're reborn in a place of loss... or if they return to the human realm, they're witless...

But take some woman or man who does approach an ascetic or brahmin to ask: 'Sir, what is skillful and what is unskillful? What is blameworthy and what is blameless? What should be cultivated and what should not be cultivated? What kind of action will lead to my lasting harm and suffering? Or what kind of action will lead to my lasting welfare and happiness?' Because of undertaking such deeds, when their body breaks up, after death, they're reborn in a good place, a heavenly realm. If they're not reborn in a heavenly realm, but return to the human realm, then wherever they're reborn they're very wise. For asking questions of ascetics or brahmins is the path leading to wisdom. (o)

So it is the way people live that makes them how they are, whether short-lived or long-lived, sickly or healthy, ugly or lovely, insignificant or illustrious, poor or rich, in a low class or eminent family, or witless or wise.

Sentient beings are the owners of their deeds and heir to their deeds. Deeds are their womb, their relative, and their refuge. It is deeds that divide beings into inferior and superior."

When he had spoken, Subha said to him, "Excellent, Mister Gotama! Excellent! As if he were righting the overturned, or revealing the hidden, or pointing out the path to the lost, or lighting a lamp in the dark so people with clear eyes can see what's there, Mister Gotama has made the Teaching clear in many ways. I go for refuge to Mister Gotama, to the teaching, and to the mendicant Sangha. From this day forth, may Mister Gotama remember me as a lay follower who has gone for refuge for life."[4] (ooo)

---

4. Middle Discourses. 135: The Shorter Analysis of Deeds.

# 12. OFFERING A MEAL TO THE BUDDHAS AND BODHISATTVAS

(Each Buddhist makes the mudra of peace with the right hand and holds it before the middle of their forehead while the left hand holds up the bowl in front of the right hand.)

**We offer this food to:**

**The Buddha Vairocana, the pure Dharma body**

**The Buddha Locana, perfected retribution body**

**The Buddha Shakyamuni, the transformation body, which is always and everywhere.**

**The Buddha Maitreya yet to be born**

**The Buddha Amitabha of the land of Great Happiness**

**All the Buddhas in the Ten Directions and the Three Times.**

**Bodhisattva Manjushri of Great Wisdom**

**Bodhisattva Samantabhadra of Great Action**

**Bodhisattva Avalokita of Great Compassion**

**Bodhisattva Mahasthamaprapta of Great Strength**

**All Bodhisattva Mahasattvas.**

**All beings in all the Dharma realms want to**

https://suttacentral.net/mn135/en/sujato

make this offering of the Three Virtues and the Six Tastes to the Buddha, Dharma and Sangha.

As we eat this food, we want all beings to realize perfectly the wisdom of awakening. (ooo)

Offering food of color, fragrance, and taste

First to the Buddhas of the ten directions

Then to the sages and saints

And also, to the beings of the six realms

Given equally without discrimination

Fulfilling all wishes abundantly.

May the Donors attain Immeasurable Perfections (Paramitas). (o)

Three virtues and six flavors

Offering to the Buddha and the Sangha

To all sentient beings in the Dharma realm offering universally. (o)

Namo the Universal Offering Bodhisattva Mahasattva. (3 times) (ooo)

# 13. OFFERING PORRIDGE AND MILK TO UNBORN BABIES

*(At the altar for the unborn child,
light incense, milk…)*

Leader:

**The Western Pure Land blessing the unborn child.** (o)

**Today, on the date of……, the bereaved family named………………. We hold a ceremony for the unborn child named……, with the Dharma name………. along with all the spirits registered at Huong Sen Temple. Inviting the soul comes at the Buddha and bows three times.** (the family bows three times) (ooo)

**Namo the Western Pure Land,
the Great Compassionate Amitabha Buddha,
blessing the unborn child.** (o)

## FIRST INVITING

Leader:  **The first inviting of the Spirit of the unborn child, descend.** (o)

**Fragrant flowers to welcome, fragrant flowers to invite.** (o)

Congregation:

**Namo summon at temple hall to listen to Dharma and enjoy the offerings of the altar.** (o)

**What is the sign of the fetus' spirit?**

**The dream has faded since many autumns.**

**Sometimes resides in the sea or dunes.**

**The soul pains alone in nowhere.**

**The incense has just been burned**

**and the Dharma word is uttered.**

**Fragrant smoke spreads throughout the mountains,**

**rivers, fields, streams, and ghostly forests.**

**The first version of the jade flower**

**With the cup of pure water**

**May the souls from all walks of life come back quickly.** (o)

**We sincerely pray, relying on the power of the Triple Gem and the secret mantras,**

**That you may come in this moment to enjoy the offerings of the altar,**

**We sincerely offer this simple ceremony for you.** (3 times) (o)

## SECOND INVITING

Leader: **The second inviting of the Spirit of the unborn child, descend. (o)**

**Fragrant flowers to welcome, fragrant flowers to invite. (o)**

Congregation:

**Namo summon at temple hall to listen to Dharma and enjoy the offerings of the altar.**

**Each essence of the Buddha emits
a bright cloud**

**Illuminating all of space with a great sound**

**Shining upon dark places**

**Eradicating all the suffering of hell. (o)**

**Today, on this auspicious day of the good month**

**With offerings of fragrant flowers**

**Unborn child, even if far away**

**Rely on the power of the Triple Gem to come and hear the Dharma. (o)**

**We sincerely pray, relying on the power of the Triple Gem and the secret mantras,**

**That you may come in this moment to enjoy the offerings of the altar,**

**With sincerity we offer this simple ceremony for you. (3 times) (o)**

## THIRD INVITING

Leader:  **The third inviting of the Spirit of the unborn child to descend. (o)**

**Fragrant flowers to welcome, fragrant flowers to invite. (o)**

Congregation:

**Nine months of pregnancy, three days of resting in one place.**

**Hoping for a harmonious life, dreaming of a happy union.**

**Good news was soon to come, but in a moment, fate intervened.**

**Jade and stone not yet distinguished, the child has departed to the nine springs.**

**Alas! The flower in its bloom, battered by the wind and rain.**

**The moon fully round, obscured by clouds.**

**Thus are the unborn children, victims of birth-related calamities, a kind of lonely soul. (o)**

**We sincerely pray, relying on the power of the Triple Gem and the secret mantras,**

**That you may come in this moment to enjoy the offerings of the altar,**

**With sincerity we offer this simple ceremony for you. (3 times) (ooo)**

**Our sincere invitation has been made**

**Your presence to witness our deep love.**

**With the initial ceremony,
we offer two jade cups,**

**Sitting briefly among the floral altar
to listen to the Dharma.**

**Namo the Great Saint who saves from the dark realms, the Honored One of Great Vows, Ksitigarbha Bodhisattva Mahasattva.**

(3 times) (o)

**Namo Amitabha Buddha**. (3 times) (o)

**At this moment, we conduct the offering
ceremony of food.** (o)

**Reverently offering to the Buddhas
in the ten directions.**

**Reverently offering to the Bodhisattvas
and all the Holy Sages.**

**Reverently offering to the Devas and spirits.**

**We lovingly offer pure food to the unborn child
and the spirits in the spiritual realm.** (o)

(The family pours milk into 3 small cups and stirs 3 bowls of porridge, inviting the unborn child to partake.)

May the unborn children receive and be full of
the offerings,

Listen to the Dharma and awaken
to the teachings,

Develop a reverence and faith in the Buddha,

Rely on the Triple Gem, practice diligently to
escape suffering.

Namo Preferred Offering Merit Bodhisattva
Mahasattva. (3 times) (o)

# 14. THE INSIGHT THAT BRINGS US TO THE OTHER SHORE

**The Heart of Prajnaparamita (Perfect Wisdom)**

Avalokiteshvara while practicing deeply with
the insight that brings us to the other shore,
suddenly discovered that all of the five skandhas
are equally empty, and with this realization he
overcame all ill-being (suffering). (o)

Listen Sariputra, this body itself is emptiness
and emptiness itself is this body.

This body is not other than emptiness and
emptiness is not other than this body.

The same is true of feelings, perceptions, mental

formations, and consciousness. (o)

Listen Sariputra, all phenomena bear the mark of emptiness; their true nature is the nature of neither birth nor death, neither being nor nonbeing, neither defilement nor purity, neither increasing nor decreasing. (o)

That is why in emptiness, body, feelings, perceptions, mental formations and consciousness are not separate self-entities.

The Eighteen Realms of Phenomena which are the six sense organs, six sense objects, and six consciousnesses are also not separate self-entities. (o)

The Twelve Links of Interdependent Arising and their extinction are also not separate self-entities. ill-being, the causes of ill-being, the end of ill-being, the path, insight and attainment, are also not separate self-entities.

Whoever can see this no longer needs to attain anything. (o)

Bodhisattvas who practice the insight that brings us to the other shore see no more obstacles in their mind, and because there are no more obstacles in their mind, they can overcome all fear, destroy all wrong perceptions and realize Perfect Nirvana.

All Buddhas in the past, present and future by

practicing the insight that brings us to the other shore, are all capable of attaining authentic and perfect enlightenment. (o)

Therefore, Sariputra, it should be known that the Insight that Brings Us to the Other Shore is a great mantra, the most illuminating mantra, the highest mantra, a mantra beyond compare, the True Wisdom that has the power to put an end to all kinds of suffering. (o)

Therefore, let us proclaim a mantra. To praise the Insight that Brings Us to the Other Shore.

Gone, gone, gone beyond, gone to the other shore, awake, rejoice! (3 times) (o)

Namo the Great Compassionate Avalokiteshvara Bodhisattva. (3 times) (ooo)

# 15. READ THE NAMES OF BUDDHAS & BODHISATTVAS

The river of attachment is ten thousand miles long.

The waves on the ocean of confusion stretch so far.

If you wish to go beyond the realms of samsara Recollect the Buddha with one pointed mind. (o)

**The Pure Land is available in our True Mind.**

**Amitabha manifests from the true nature
of things,**

**Shining light on the three worlds and the
ten directions,**

**Always abiding in the present moment.** (o)

**May I return to Amitabha Buddha**

**The founder of the Pure Land**

**The source of limitless lifespan.**

**May I with one heart visualize**

**And recollect this holy name.**

**Namo Amitabhaya Buddhaya, the Buddha of
Infinite Light.** (3 times) (o)

**Namo Manjushri, the Bodhisattva of Great
Understanding.** (3 times) (o)

**Namo Samantabhadra, the Bodhisattva of
Great Action.** (3 times) (o)

**Namo Avalokiteshvara, the Bodhisattva of
Great Compassion.** (3 times) (o)

**Namo Kshitigarbhaya Bodhisattvaya, the
Bodhisattva of Great Aspiration.** (3 times) (o)

# 16. REPENTANT VERSE FOR THE UNBORN CHILD

Respectfully to the Buddhas, Bodhisattvas,
and Holy Sages,

Please bestow your compassionate blessings,
to witness the disciples. (o)

Directed towards the unborn children

In this life and past lives

Whether you are our own

Or of our parents

Or of all people.

We, either directly or indirectly

Have harmed the unborn children

Expressing our heartfelt sorrow

We sincerely repent. (o)

Oh, unborn children

Please understand

With tears in our eyes,

We sincerely repent. (o)

You are also flesh and blood

Enduring immense pain

Being cut and torn apart

Limbs and body. (o)

Unjustly suffering
Some were poisoned
Ending your lives
Or suffocated
Drowning to a wrongful death
In many ways
Out of ignorance and lack of virtue
The sins are enormous. (o)
We bow and repent
Asking for forgiveness
Parents in ignorance
Driven by attachment
Committed these sins.
Now, earnestly,
Before the unborn children
We sincerely repent
Knowing these sins
Are not easily forgiven. (o)
Now, relying on the Buddha
We ask the spirits of the unborn children
To understand our hearts
And follow the Buddha's teachings. (o)
Receive the merit of offerings

**To save the spirits of the unborn children**

**From places of suffering**

**Take refuge in the Triple Gem**

**Arouse the Bodhi mind**

**Aspire to become Buddhas.** (o)

**From now on**

**We vow to create good conditions**

**To be disciples of the Buddha**

**In this life and future lives.** (o)

**Abandon evil and do good**

**Be kind to each other**

**Rely on the Triple Gem**

**And aspire for the supreme path.** [5] (o)

**Namo the Repentance Bodhisattva.** (3 times) (o)

---

5. Kệ sám Thai Nhi. Vietnamese from Website, the Ba vàng Temple.
https://chuabavang.com/bai-2-cau-sieu-vong-linh-thai-nhi-tai-nha- khong-ve-chua-lam-le-cau-sieu-duoc-d2478.html
"Repentant Verse For The Unborn Child," English translation by Thich Nu Gioi Huong

# 17. BLESSING VERSE FOR THE DECEASED

On the sacred altar, the incense smoke
rises thickly

Our sincere hearts fervently from this moment

The five-colored auspicious clouds surround

Protecting humanity, including many
suffering souls. (o)

We know the saying "Death is a return;
Life is a journey"

For people in this world, who can live long?

Because of deep obligations
and profound kindness

Care for our fellow beings, sharing
the same source. (o)

Born in misfortune during the
Dharma-declining age

Enduring countless misery

In life, facing hardships and turmoil

In death, bodies incomplete, handed over
to the death god. (o)

Now we wholeheartedly pray

Asking the Buddha to mercifully save the souls

Relying on the enlightened Buddhas

To pity the impermanent human lives. (o)

Where there is birth, there is sorrow

In the cycle of samsara, many paths lead
to disasters

Forms exist and perish, nothing is permanent

The transitory nature of existence is evident.

Even if one has wealth and beauty for a
hundred years

This fleeting life is not easily extended

Troubled souls wander aimlessly.

Listen to the scriptures and chants for rebirth. (o)

Quickly take refuge in the Triple Gem

The water from the willow branch washes away
worldly dust

Absorbing the profound grace of the Buddha

All obstacles and sins gradually dissipate.

Now is the time for the soul to leave
behind illusions

Quickly return to the pure land of the
Western Paradise

Souls rely on the fragrant incense smoke

Day and night enjoying the tranquility
of the Pure Land. (ooo)

# 18. TAKING REFUGE
# IN AMITABHA BUDDHA

Taking refuge in the Amitabha Buddha

In the wondrous ultimate dimension,

We devote our heart to returning to myself

And holding to the source of mindfulness.

We have vowed to go for refuge
to the Amitabha Buddha. (o)

We bow our heads and ask the Buddha

To receive us in his embrace.

As the Pure Land manifests,

Please bring your torch of light

To shine onto our thoughts.

Please bring the boat of long lifespan

To carry our body through life

So we live with peace and joy,

So our aspiration can be fully realized.

Buddha, please always protect us. (o)

Not letting our mind grow slack,

So that we end wrong perceptions

And the affliction falls away.

In the present moment

Buddha can be found in this world.

Taking every step with solidity and freedom
We walk in the Pure Land.
When we live the present moment mindfully,
The Pure Land is already a reality.
So whatever form we take in the future,
We can be assured of peace and joy. (o)
If we are able to recollect the Amitabha
With undispersed, one-pointed mind,
The nine lotus grades will appear.
May we enjoy life for ourselves and others
And know in advance our time of death.
At death may our mind not flinch,
Our body not be sick and in pain,
Our thoughts not waiver. (o)
May the Amitabha and his holy assembly
Holding up the golden lotuses
Be present without delay.
Together may we set out in freedom
May we see the Buddha in the opening lotus.
May the Pure Land be our home.
I bow my head to ask Buddha to be my witness
To my never-slackening practice. (o)
Namo Amitabha Buddha (3 times) (ooo)

# 19. ENCOURAGEMENT TO PRACTICE

Today has already passed

Our lifespan and blood gradually dry up

Like fish in a drying pond

Suffering increases with no joy at all.

We must practice to save ourselves quickly like
the fire burning on heads.

Do not waste time as if attending a royal court

Knowing that the body is fragile
and impermanent

Present in the morning but death by the evening

Focus on saving yourself. (o)

# 20. SHARING THE MERIT
# & VERSE FOR CLOSING

Reciting the sutras, practicing the way of
awareness gives rise to benefits without limit.

We vow to share the fruits with all beings.

We vow to offer tribute to parents, teachers,
friends, and numerous beings who give
guidance and support along the path. (o)

May we be born now in the Pure Land within
the heart of a lotus flower.

**In the moment when the lotus blooms, we touch the reality of no-birth and no-dying.**

**May Buddhas and Bodhisattvas be our companions on the wonderful path of practice.** (o)

**May we end all afflictions so that understanding can arise, the obstacles of unwholesome acts be dissolved, and the fruit of awakening be fully realized.** (o)

**Namo Amitabha Buddhaya.** (3 times) (ooo)

# 21. PRESENTING THE WISHES

Leader:

Namo the Lord of the Underworld, Savior from Suffering, Honored One, Deliverer from Dark Realms, Great Vow Ksitigarbha Bodhisattva.

Namo the Triple Gem, Bodhisattvas, celestial beings, Brahma King, Indra, and the Four Heavenly Kings, the Eight Divisions of Heavenly Dragons, Dharma Protectors, and all benevolent deities who compassionately prove and protect us.

Today, dated......... We, (*the ritual leader: Bhikṣuṇī...*) together with the families of the unborn children and the Buddhist devotees of Huong Sen Temple, Perris, California, sincerely conduct the prayer for the unborn babies. We recite sutras (*such as the Sutras of Loving-kindness, Consequences of Good and Evil Deeds, Karmic Retribution of Hungry Ghosts, Longevity and Shortened Life)*, invoke the Buddhas' and Bodhisattvas' names, make offerings, and transfer the merits to unborn babies amd twelve kinds of named or unnamed souls.

We would like dedicate the merit from this ceremony, along with other merits generated by the family and relatives, for the unborn babies... (*name, Dharma name, age*), as well as other spirits registered at Huong Sen Temple, all the twelve types of lonely spirits, and the deceased ancestors from many past lives of our families to rebirth peacefully in the new land. We pray for these beings to increase in blessings and wisdom, to rely on the Triple Gem for practice, and to soon achieve enlightenment and liberation. (o)

Finally, may all sentient beings soon complete the Way of Love and Understanding.

*The sangha reads together*: Namo Amitabha Buddha. (ooo)

# 22. TAKING REFUGE AT THE THREE JEWELS

- I take refuge in the Buddha

the one who shows me the way in this life.

I take refuge in the Dharma

the way of understanding and of love.

I take refuge in the Sangha

the community that lives in harmony and

awareness. (o) (1 prostration)

- Dwelling in the refuge of Buddha

I clearly see the path of light and beauty
in the world.

Dwelling in the refuge of Dharma

I learn to open many doors on the path
of transformation.

Dwelling in the refuge of Sangha

shining light that supports me, keeping my

practice free of obstruction. (o) (1 prostration)


- Taking refuge in the Buddha in myself

I aspire to help all people recognize their own

awakened nature, realizing the Mind of Love.

Taking refuge in the Dharma in myself

I aspire to help all people fully master the ways of practice and walk together on the path of liberation.

Taking refuge in the Sangha in myself

I aspire to help all people build Fourfold Communities,

to embrace all beings and support their transformation. (ooo) (1 prostration)

# 23. SALUTATION TO THOUSANDS OF BUDDHAS IN THREE TIMES

There are many the great causes

The ten directions, three lives and realms

I keep my body and mind pure

Pay homage at all without being left behind. (o)

We pay respects sincerely to the four graces of the three realms:

Namo the Buddhas of the kalpa thousands in the past. (o) (1 prostration)

Namo the Buddhas of the kalpa thousands in the present. (o) (1 prostration)

Namo the Buddhas of the kalpa thousands in the future. (o) (1 prostration)

# 24. THE DIVINE GATHA

Gods, nagas, asuras and yakshas
Come here, with all your heart listen
to the Dharma.
Protect the Buddha-dharma so that it
may endure
And all may act in the spirit of the
Buddha's teaching.

When you have come to hear the Dharma
Whether you are under the earth or in the sky
Look at all beings with the eyes of love
Day and night abide in the right practice.

May the world always be safe and secure
Impregnated by the merit of wisdom and love.
May all the obstacles of wrongdoing be dissolved.
May we leave behind afflictions
and know always how to touch peace and joy.

May the Sangha with determination observe
the precepts

**Be diligent in the practice of meditative concentration.**

**May the flower of awakened understanding bloom beautifully**

**And everywhere may all species have happiness.**

**Namo the Dharma Protective Bodhisattva Mahasattva.** (3 times) (ooo)

# BAO ANH LAC BOOKSHELF
## Dr. Bhikṣuṇī TN Giới Hương composed

### 1.1. THE VIETNAMESE BOOKS

1. *Bồ-tát và Tánh Không Trong Kinh Tạng Pali và Đại Thừa* (Boddhisattva and Sunyata in the Early and Developed Buddhist Traditions).

2. *Ban Mai Xứ Ấn* (The Dawn in India) - *Tuyển tập các Tiểu Luận Phật Giáo* (Collection of Buddhist Essays), (3 tập).

3. *Sārnātha - Vườn Nai – Chiếc Nôi Phật Giáo* (Sārnātha - Deer Park–The Cradle of Buddhism).

4. *Quy Y Tam Bảo và Năm Giới* (Take Refuge in Three Gems and Keep the Five Precepts).

5. *Vòng Luân Hồi* (The Cycle of Life).

6. *Hoa Tuyết Milwaukee* (Snowflake in Milwaukee).

7. *Luân Hồi trong Lăng Kính Lăng Nghiêm* (The Rebirth in Śūrangama Sūtra).

8. *Nghi Thức Hộ Niệm, Cầu Siêu* (The Ritual for the Deceased).

9. *Quan Âm Quảng Trần* (The Commentary of Avalokiteśvara Bodhisattva).

10. *Nữ Tu và Tù Nhân Hoa Kỳ* (A Nun and American Inmates).

11. *Nếp Sống Tỉnh Thức của Đức Đạt Lai Lạt Ma Thứ XIV*

(The Awakened Mind of the 14th Dalai Lama).

12. *A-Hàm: Mưa pháp chuyển hóa phiền não (Agama – A Dharma Rain transforms the Defilement)*, 2 tập.

13. *Góp Từng Hạt Nắng Perris* (Collection of Sunlight in Perris).

14. *Pháp Ngữ của Kinh Kim Cang* (The Key Words of Vajracchedikā-Prajñāpāramitā-Sūtra).

15. *Tập Thơ Nhạc Nắng Lăng Nghiêm* (Songs and Poems of Śūraṅgama Sunlight).

16. *Nét Bút Bên Song Cửa* (Reflections at the Temple Window).

17. *Máy Nghe MP3 Hương Sen* (Hương Sen Digital Mp3 Radio Speaker): Các Bài Giảng, Sách, Bài viết và Thơ Nhạc của Thích Nữ Giới Hương (383/201 bài).

18. *DVD Giới Thiệu về Chùa* Hương Sen, USA (Introduction on Huong Sen Temple).

19. *Ni Giới Việt Nam Hoằng Pháp tại Hoa Kỳ* (Sharing the Dharma - Vietnamese Buddhist Nuns in the United States).

20. *Tuyển Tập 40 Năm Tu Học & Hoằng Pháp của Ni sư Giới* Hương (Forty Years in the Dharma: A Life of Study and Service—Venerable Bhikkhuni Giới Hương), Thích Nữ Viên Quang, TN Viên Nhuận, TN Viên Tiến, and TN Viên Khuông.

21. *Tập Thơ Nhạc Lối Về Sen Nở (Songs and Poems of Lotus Blooming on the Way)*.

22. *Nghi Thức Công Phu Khuya – Thần Chú Thủ Lăng Nghiêm* (Śūraṅgama Mantra).

23. *Nghi Thức Cầu An – Kinh Phổ Môn* (The Universal Door Sūtra).

24. *Nghi Thức Cầu An – Kinh Dược Sư* (The Medicine Buddha Sūtra).

25. *Nghi Thức Sám Hối Hồng Danh* (The Sūtra of Confession at many Buddha Titles).

26. *Nghi Thức* Công Phu *Chiều – Mông* Sơn *Thí Thực* (The Ritual Donating Food to Hungry Ghosts).

27. *Khóa Tịnh* Độ *– Kinh A Di* Đà (The Amitabha Buddha Sūtra).

28. *Nghi Thức Cúng Linh và Cầu Siêu* (The Rite for Deceased and Funeral Home).

29. *Nghi Lễ Hàng Ngày - 50 Kinh Tụng và các Lễ Vía trong Năm* (The Daily Chanting Rituals and Annual Ceremonies).

30. *Hương Đạo Trong* Đời *2022* (Tuyển tập 60 Bài Thi trong Cuộc Thi Viết Văn Ứng Dụng Phật Pháp 2022 - A Collection of Writings on the Practicing of Buddhism in Daily Life in the Writing Contest 2022).

31. *Hương Pháp 2022* (Tuyển Tập Các Bài Thi Trúng Giải Cuộc Thi Viết Văn Ứng Dụng Phật Pháp 2022 - A Collection of the Winning Writings on the Practicing of Buddhism in Daily Life in the Writing Contest 2022).

32. *Giới Hương - Thơm Ngược Gió Ngàn* (Giới Hương – The Virtue Fragrance Against the Thousand Winds), Nguyên Hà.

33. *Pháp Ngữ Kinh Hoa Nghiêm* (Buddha-avatamsaka-nāma-mahāvaipulya-sūtra) (2 tập).

34. *Tinh Hoa Kinh Hoa Nghiêm (The Core of Buddha-avatamsaka-nāma-mahāvaipulya-sūtra).*

35. *Phật Giáo – Tầm Nhìn Lịch Sử Và Thực Hành (Buddhism: A Historical and Practical Vision).* Hiệu đính: Thích

Hạnh Chánh và Thích Nữ Giới Hương.

## 1.2. THE ENGLISH BOOKS

1. *Boddhisattva and Sunyata in the Early and Developed Buddhist Traditions.*

2. *Rebirth Views in the Śūraṅgama Sūtra.*

3. *Commentary of Avalokiteśvara Bodhisattva.*

4. *The Key Words in Vajracchedikā Sūtra.*

5. *Sārnātha-The Cradle of Buddhism in the Archeological View.*

6. *Take Refuge in the Three Gems and Keep the Five Precepts.*

7. *Cycle of Life.*

8. *Forty Years in the Dharma: A Life of Study and Service— Venerable Bhikkhuni Giới Hương.*

9. *Sharing the Dharma -Vietnamese Buddhist Nuns in the United States.*

10. *A Vietnamese Buddhist Nun and American Inmates.*

11. *Daily Monastic Chanting.*

12. *Weekly Buddhist Discourse Chanting.*

13. *Practice Meditation and Pure Land.*

14. *The Ceremony for Peace.*

15. *The Lunch Offering Ritual.*

16. *The Ritual Offering Food to Hungry Ghosts.*

17. *The Pureland Course of Amitabha Sutra.*

18. *The Medicine Buddha Sutra.*

19. *The New Year Ceremony.*

20. *The Great Parinirvana Ceremony.*

21. *The Buddha's Birthday Ceremony.*

22. *The Ullambana Festival (Parents' Day).*

23. *The Marriage Ceremony.*

24. *The Blessing Ceremony for The Deceased.*

25. *The Ceremony Praising Ancestral Masters.*

26. *The Enlightened Buddha Ceremony.*

27. *The Uposatha Ceremony (Reciting Precepts).*

28. *Buddhism: A Historical and Practical Vision.* Edited by Ven. Dr. Thich Hanh Chanh and Ven. Dr. Bhikṣuṇī TN Gioi Huong.

29. *Contribution of Buddhism For World Peace & Social Harmony.* Edited by Ven. Dr. Buddha Priya Mahathero and Ven. Dr. Bhikṣuṇī TN Gioi Huong.

30. *Global Spread of Buddhism with Special Reference to Sri Lanka.* Buddhist Studies Seminar in Kandy University. Edited by Dr. Ven. Kahawatte Siri Sumedha Thero and Dr. Bhikṣuṇī TN Gioi Huong.

31. *Buddhism In Sri Lanka During The Period of 19th to 21st Centuries.* Buddhist Studies Seminar in Colombo. Edited by Prof. Ven. Medagama Nandawansa and Dr. Bhikṣuṇī TN Gioi Huong.

32. *Diary: Practicing Vipassana and the Four Foundations of Mindfulness Sutta.*

33. *Prayer for the Souls of Unborn Babies.*

### 1.3. THE BILINGUAL BOOKS (VIETNAMESE-ENGLISH)

1. *Bản Tin Hương Sen: Xuân, Phật Đản, Vu Lan (*Hương Sen Newsletter: Spring, Buddha Birthday and Vu Lan, annual/ Mỗi Năm).

2. *Danh Ngôn Nuôi Dưỡng Nhân Cách - Good Sentences*

*Nurture a Good Manner.*

3. *Văn Hóa Đặc Sắc của Nước Nhật Bản-Exploring the Unique Culture of Japan.*

4. *Sống An Lạc dù Đời không Đẹp như Mơ - Live Peacefully though Life is not Beautiful as a Dream.*

5. *Hãy Nói Lời Yêu Thương-Words of Love and Understanding.*

6. *Văn Hóa Cổ Kim qua Hành Hương Chiêm Bái -The Ancient- Present Culture in Pilgrim.*

7. *Nghệ Thuật Biết Sống - Art of Living.*

8. *Dharamshala - Hành Hương Vùng Đất Thiêng, Ấn Độ, Dharamshala - Pilgrimage to the Sacred Land, India.*

## 1.4. THE TRANSLATED BOOKS

1. *Xá Lợi Của Đức Phật* (Relics of the Buddha), Tham Weng Yew.

2. *Sen Nở Nơi Chốn Tử Tù* (Lotus in Prison), many authors.

3. *Chùa Việt Nam Hải Ngoại* (Overseas Vietnamese Buddhist Temples).

4. *Việt Nam Danh Lam Cổ Tự* (The Famous Ancient Buddhist Temples in Vietnam).

5. *Hương Sen, Thơ và Nhạc* – (Lotus Fragrance, Poem and Music).

6. *Phật Giáo-Một Bậc Đạo Sư, Nhiều Truyền Thống* (Buddhism: One Teacher – Many Traditions), Đức Đạt Lai Lạt Ma 14th & Ni Sư Thubten Chodren.

7. *Cách Chuẩn Bị Chết và Giúp Người Sắp Chết-Quan Điểm Phật Giáo* (Preparing for Death and Helping the Dying – A Buddhist Perspective).

## 2.BUDDHIST MUSIC ALBUMS
## from POEMS of THÍCH NỮ GIỚI HƯƠNG

1. *Đào Xuân Lộng Ý Kinh* (The Buddha's Teachings Reflected in Cherry Flowers).

2. *Niềm Tin Tam Bảo* (Trust in the Three Gems).

3. *Trăng Tròn Nghìn Năm Đón Chờ Ai* (Who Is the Full Moon Waiting for for Over a Thousand Years?).

4. *Ánh Trăng Phật Pháp* (Moonlight of Dharma-Buddha).

5. *Bình Minh Tỉnh Thức* (Awakened Mind at the Dawn) (*Piano Variations for Meditation*).

6. *Tiếng Hát Già Lam* (Song from Temple).

7. *Cảnh Đẹp Chùa Xưa* (The Magnificent, Ancient Buddhist Temple).

8. *Karaoke Hoa Ưu Đàm Đã Nở* (An Udumbara Flower Is Blooming).

9. *Hương Sen Ca* (Hương Sen's Songs)

10. *Về Chùa Vui Tu* (Happily Go to Temple for Spiritual Practices)

11. *Gọi Nắng Xuân Về* (Call the Spring Sunlight).

12. Đệ *Tử Phật*. Thơ: Thích Nữ Giới Hương, Nhạc: Uy Thi Ca & Giác An, volume 4, năm 2023.


Mời xem:

http://www.huongsentemple.com/index.php/kinh-sach/tu-sach-bao-anh-lac